For Em and BJ...

Proverbs 18:16

Copyright ©2011, ©2012 by Dana Todd Pope

Cover Design by Dana Todd Pope
Book Design by Dana Todd Pope

All rights reserved.  All international rights reserved.

No part of this book may be reproduced in any form or by electronic or mechanical means, including storage and retrieval systems, without permission in writing from the author.

This book was printed by CreateSpace.com.

Dana Todd Pope
For more information, visit DanaToddPope.com.

Made in the United States of America

First printing:  September 2012
Second printing: July 2016

ISBN:  978-0-9883868-1-5

The Budding Mogul Club™ Presents:

# "Know Money, GROW Money."™

Written and Illustrated by **Dana Todd Pope**

Copyright ©2011, ©2012 Dana Todd Pope

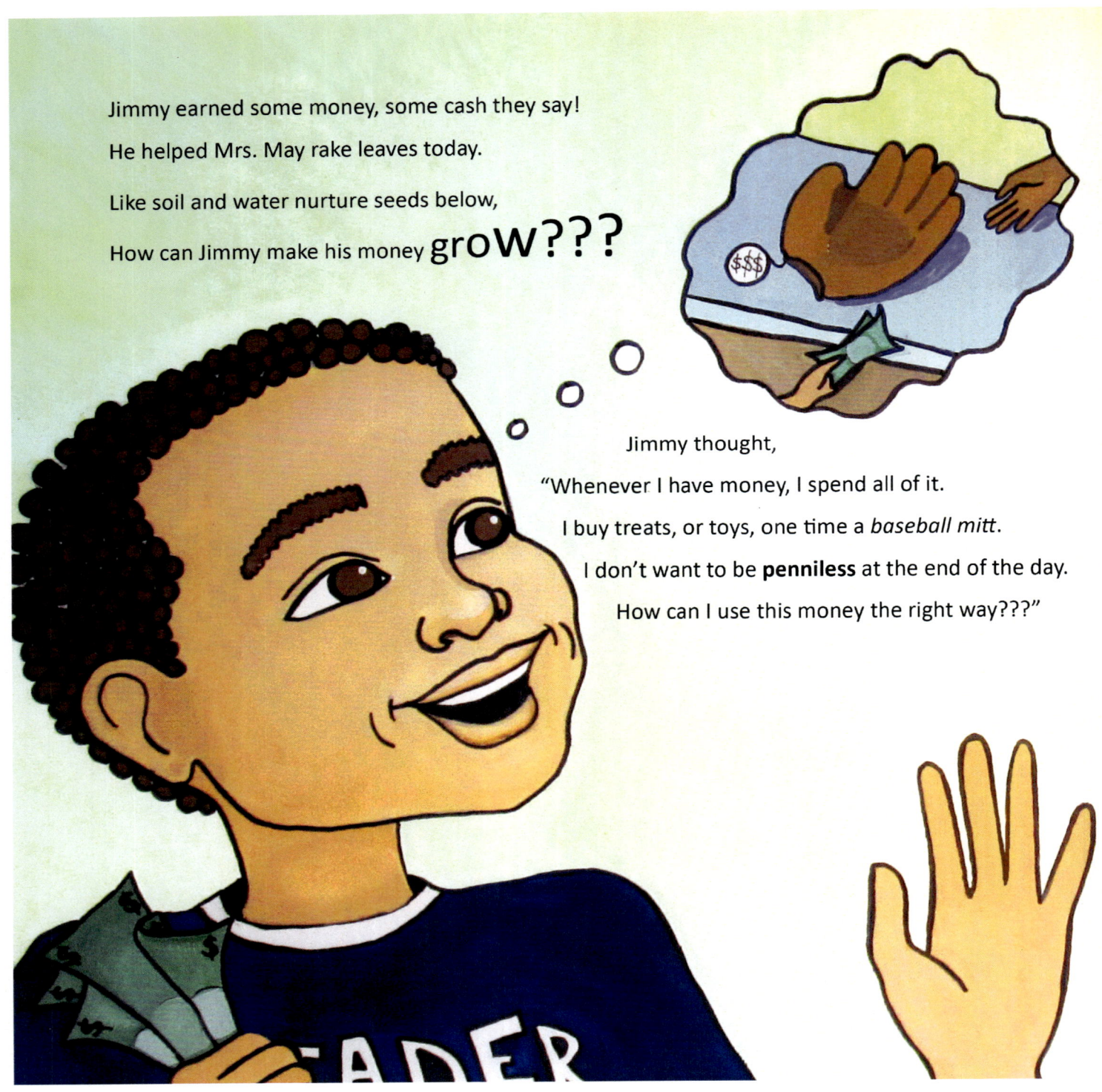

"I'll ask Mrs. Reed. She should know.

She can help me make my money gr**OW**.

There she is coming down the street.

I'll walk toward her until our paths meet."

Jimmy said, "Hi Mrs. Reed, good day to you.

Aren't you a banker, isn't that true?"

She said, "Yes Jimmy, indeed it's true.

Banking is what I love to do."

Jimmy said, "Well, I earned some money raking leaves.

Do you have time to answer a question please?"

She said, "I'm picking up an egg biscuit with cheese.

Walk with me and enjoy this morning breeze."

Jimmy said, "When I have money, I spend all of it.

I buy treats, or toys, sometimes a *ball to hit*.

I don't want to be penniless by the end of the day.

How can I use this money the right way???"

She replied, "You can save or lend,

**Invest** or spend... It all depends.

'Work smart, then hard,' is what I always say.

Take your time, think it out and you'll find a way."

"In my personal opinion, the best thing to do
Is to invest your money so it can work for you.
Open a bank account then learn ways to invest.
Go to the **library** where you can plan the rest."

Jimmy said, "Thanks," and said "Goodbye,"
then decided to give the library a try.
Just then, he saw Pastor Dinks.
Jimmy thought, "I wonder what he thinks?"

"Whenever I have money, I spend all of it.
I buy treats or toys... *I will admit*.
I don't want to be penniless by the end of the day.
How can I use my money the right way???"

"Well little Jimmy" the Pastor replied,
"Being smart with your money is indeed wise.
Make sure you **tithe** at least 10 percent
Of your money before any is spent."

"Some people call it a seed you sow.
God will guide you to make the rest gr**ow**.
Pray over your **stewardship** both night and day
And **commit** to use your money in the best way."

"Thank you Pastor" Jimmy said with a smile.
Jimmy found both **insights** as truly worthwhile.
Well, off to the library to write his money plan.
Oh look!  Here comes his friend Jan.

Jan said, "I heard you made some cash. What's new?"
"Did you buy the new Zii-Bot 2?"
Jimmy said, "No way,
I'm off to make financial plans."
Come with me to help, if you can?"

Jan said yes and they headed down the street.
Jimmy and Jan had no idea who next they would meet.
It was Will Waites a **billionaire entrepreneur**!!!!!
He wrote a new book and was on the promotion tour.

Mr. Waites was getting in his limo when they saw something drop.

It was Mr. Waites' wallet so they asked him to stop.

He was so grateful his wallet was returned,

He asked what they wanted for the favor they had earned.

Jimmy said, "Whenever I get money, I spend all of it.
I buy treats, or toys, sometimes *a magic kit*.
I don't want to be penniless by the end of the day.
How can I use my money the right way???"

"Well little Jimmy, you're on the right track."
Mr. Waites said as he patted Jimmy on the back.
"I'm glad you're so young and at this stage.
When I was a boy, I was on the same page.

Careful planning of your dollars is the way to go.
If you plan a little well, a lot can gr**OW**.
Find your **passion** and it will lead you to success.
Never stop learning and always do your best.
Take my card. I will **mentor** you, keep in touch."

"Absolutely Mr. Waites, thank you so much!"
Jimmy replied feeling excited and full of joy.
Now there were three insights for this little boy.

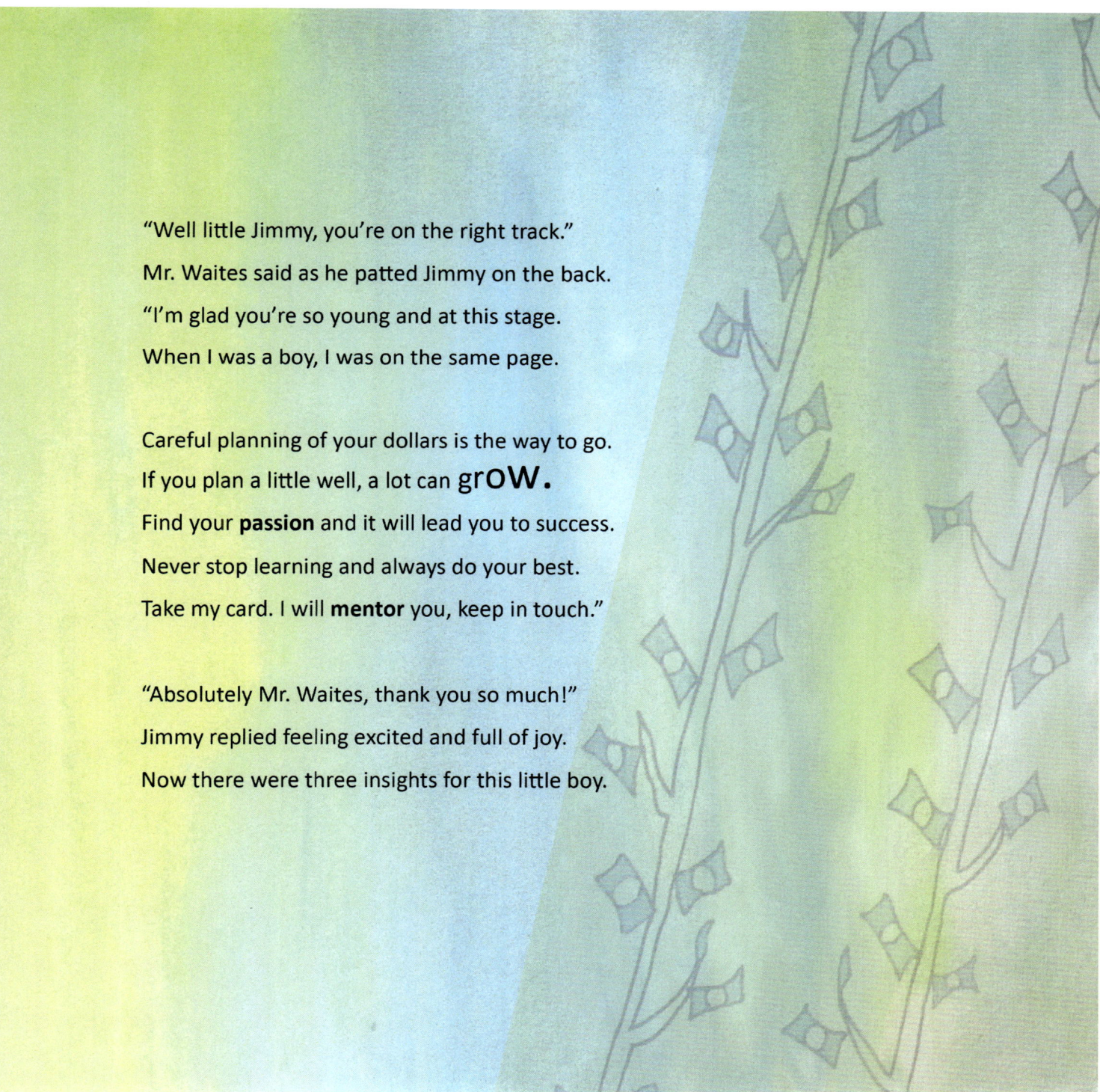

On to the library they continued to walk.

As they walked they continued to talk.

Jimmy now had so many ideas.

Oh, look at who's leaving the pizzeria!

Emory and Xave were headed to buy a Zii-bot 2.

They asked Jimmy and Jan if they were getting one, too.

Jimmy proceeded to tell them about his plan

And how one day he would be a **wealthy** man.

Jimmy said, "Whenever I get money, I spend all of it.

I buy treats, or toys, sometimes *a banana split*.

This time, I WILL have money at the end of the day.

I WILL use this money the right way!!!"

Xave replied, "I hear what you're saying,

But when the other kids are playing

With the new Zii-bot 2

What are we supposed to do?"

Jimmy was ready to respond but before he could

A homeless guy walked up wearing a hood.

He'd been listening to the whole conversation

And couldn't resist adding his notation.

The guy said, "It's good to take time to plan how you spend.

Then you won't have to look for someone to lend

You money just to cover your basic **expenses**,

Because you wasted your money **keeping up pretenses**.

I went to college, got a job… did most everything right.

I didn't save, got into debt… which led to my plight.

I got **laid off**… no job and no savings to show…

Make sure you save kids, listen to what I now know."

He then turned and staggered off to meet

Another homeless guy further down the street.

The kids appreciated the wise words that were said.

Emory and Xave changed their plans to join Jimmy instead.

On to the library they started to walk.  As they walked, they continued to talk.

They agreed to make the library their **hub** and to call themselves, "The Budding **Mogul** Club."

The library seemed HUGE with so many books.

The kids really didn't know where to look.

The librarian said, "We have books but, periodicals too.

Is this for some type of project due?"

Jimmy replied, "No, but what would you suggest?
We would like to find out which way is best
To make our money grOW and grOW.
We're here to learn what we need to know."

The librarian showed them books about investing and **strategy**.

Jan and Xave searched sites on the web randomly.

**Stocks** and **bonds** became Emory's obsession.

Jimmy thought, "Now when I get money, I'll be careful with it.

I'll tithe, invest, and always save a little bit.

This time, I still have money at the end of the day

And a plan to use it the right way!!!"

Jimmy dressed for the night then lay in his bed
Reflecting on his plan and all that was said.
He was given great advice and heeded every word.
Jimmy was grateful for every comment that he heard.
Jimmy thought, "Thanks to **Mrs. Reed, Pastor Dinks**, **Mr. Waites**, and **the guy on the street**.
I will never misuse my money, given what I now know.
With their four insights, my money is sure to grOW."

THE END

# Glossary

**Bank-** A place that holds money deposited by customers, pays it out when required, loans money to customers, collects interest from loans, and exchanges currency.

**Banker-** A person who serves as the officer or owner of a bank.

**Bankrupt-** Having no money.

**Billionaire-** A person who has money or possessions worth one billion dollars (or other currency) or more.

**Bonds-** A piece of paper a government or business gives when it borrows money. A bond promises to repay the sum of money along with interest.

**Broke-** *Informal* for having little or no money. Bankrupt. Also past tense for *break*.

**Business-** A group or company that buys and sells goods or services in order to make money. Also, the type of industry someone works in.

**Commit-** To devote, dedicate yourself, or pledge to do something.

**Entrepreneur-** A person who works for himself/ herself by assuming the risk of owning and operating one or several businesses.

**Expenses-** Money spent on the costs of living.

**Expertise-** Expert commentary or opinion. The skill or knowledge of an expert.

**Homeless-** A person who has no home of their own.

**Hub-** A central location around which activity happens.

**Invest-** To commit money to a business or venture in order to gain a profit.

**Insight-** The ability to see and understand clearly the inner nature of things.

**Keeping up Pretenses-** Pretending to do better or have more than you actually have.

**Laid off –** The act of putting a person or group of people out of work, sometimes temporarily.

# Glossary (continued)

**Library-** A place that has lots of books, records, and other materials that may be borrowed or studied.

**Mentor-** Someone who is a more knowledgeable guide or teacher to someone else. You can have different mentors to teach you different things.

**Mogul-** A powerful and very rich business person. Usually they have several successful business interests.

**Moneyless-** Having no money.

**Passion-** A strong liking for something or the object of a strong liking.

**Pastor-** The head minister in charge of a church or organization.

**Penniless-** Having no money, not even a penny.

**Periodicals-** A newspaper or magazine published at regular intervals, like once a week, monthy, etc...

**Strategy (Business Strategy)-** Method or plan used in hopes to make a business successful.

**Stewardship-** Responsible management of something someone has been trusted to care for (i.e. money).

**Stocks-** The shares or parts of ownership of a company or business.

**Talent-** A natural skill or ability.

**Tithe-** To pay or donate one tenth of one's income to a church, other religious organization or charity.

**Wealthy-** Having a large amount of money or possessions.

www.danatoddpope.com

Are you a Budding Mogul? What do you want to do?

How will you make your money grOW for you?

What is your passion, idea or **talent**?

Put your plan to paper and get started if you haven't.

## My Plan!

_____
_____
_____
_____
_____
_____
_____
_____
_____
_____
_____

Made in the USA
Lexington, KY
22 June 2018